On a Trip

by Roman Rodriguez
illustrated by Hope Julien

Practice Decodable 24

McGraw Hill Education

Bothell, WA • Chicago, IL • Columbus, OH • New York, NY

MHEonline.com

Send all inquiries to:
McGraw-Hill Education
8787 Orion Place
Columbus, OH 43240

ISBN: 978-0-02-144765-7
MHID: 0-02-144765-9

Printed in the United States of America.

7 GPC 23

Jo Had Fun

On a trip, Jo had fun.

Jo swam with Mom and Dad.

Look down, Mom!

Can you spot crabs and clams?

Mom did.

Mom was glad.

Jo Spots Cans

Look down, Dad!

Can you spot red cans?

Dad had a bag with him.
Dad can grab the red cans.

Dad can drop the cans in a bin.
Jo was glad.